12 CHRISTMAS
VOCAL SOLOS
FOR CLASSICAL SINGERS

To access companion recorded accompaniments online, visit:
www.halleonard.com/mylibrary

4322-4181-8701-1247

ISBN 978-1-4584-1379-6

G. SCHIRMER, Inc.

DISTRIBUTED BY

HAL•LEONARD®

Visit Hal Leonard Online at
www.halleonard.com

Contact us:
Hal Leonard
7777 West Bluemound Road
Milwaukee, WI 53213
Email: info@halleonard.com

In Europe, contact:
Hal Leonard Europe Limited
Dettingen Way
Bury St Edmunds, Suffolk, IP33 3YB
Email: info@halleonardeurope.com

In Australia, contact:
Hal Leonard Australia Pty. Ltd.
4 Lentara Court
Cheltenham, Victoria, 3192 Australia
Email: info@halleonard.com.au

CONTENTS

Pianist on the recordings:
Laura Ward

The price of this publication includes access to companion recorded accompaniments online, for download or streaming, using the unique code found on the title page. Visit **www.halleonard.com/mylibrary** and enter the access code.

GLORY HALLELUJAH TO DE NEW-BORN KING

(Christmas Spiritual)

African-American Spiritual
arranged by Hall Johnson

Tell me who do you call _ de

Won - der - ful Coun - sel - lor? Oh, _____ Glo - ry Hal - le - lu - jah! Oh, _____

Glo - ry Hal - le - lu - jah! Glo - ry Hal - le - lu - jah to de new - born King! _ Well,

I call Je - sus de Won - der - ful Coun - sel - or. Oh, _____

Glo - ry Hal - le - lu - jah! Oh, _____ Glo - ry Hal - le - lu - jah!

[*rit. last time*]   **Fine**

Glo - ry Hal - le - lu - jah to de new - born King. _ Jus' fol - low de Star _ an'

[*rit. last time*]

you'll find de Ba - by, Oh, _____ Glo - ry Hal - le - lu - jah! Oh, _____

Glo-ry Hal-le-lu-jah! Glo-ry Hal-le-lu-jah to de new-born King.__ You'll

find Him in Beth - le-hem wrapped in de man - ger, Oh,_____

Glo-ry Hal-le-lu-jah! Oh,_____ Glo-ry Hal-le-lu-jah!

Glo-ry Hal-le-lu-jah to de new-born King.__ Cry-in' "Peace on earth,_ good-will_

D.S. al Fine

I WONDER AS I WANDER

(Appalachian Carol)

Collected, adapted, and arranged by
John Jacob Niles

I won-der as I wan-der, out un-der the sky, How

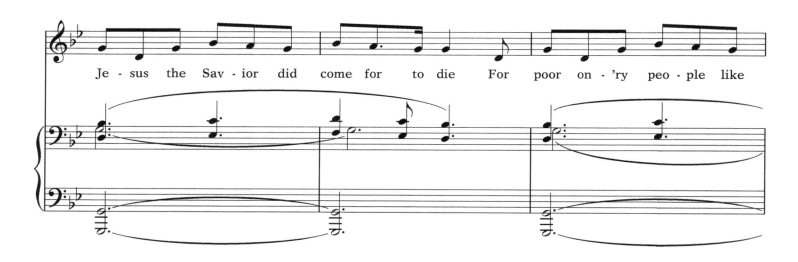

Je - sus the Sav - ior did come for to die For poor on - 'ry peo - ple like

you and like I... I won - der as I wan - der, out un - der the sky.

When Ma-ry birthed Je-sus, 'twas in a cow's stall, With

wise men and farm-ers and shep-herds and all. But high from God's heav-en a

star's light did fall, And the prom-ise of a-ges it then did re-call.

I won-der as I wan-der, out un-der the sky, How

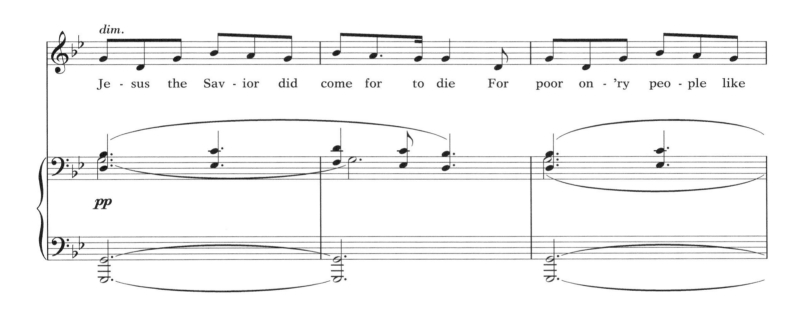

Je - sus the Sav - ior did come for to die For poor on - 'ry peo - ple like

you and like I... I won-der as I wan-der, out un-der the sky.

for Thomas Michael Tolliver Niles on being five years of age

JESUS, JESUS, REST YOUR HEAD

Adapted from the singing
of three people in Hardin County, Kentucky

Adapted by
John Jacob Niles

LULLE LULLAY

Collected and arranged by
John Jacob Niles
adapted and arranged for voice and piano by
Bryan Stanley

With graceful movement

Lul - lay, __ Thou ti - ny lit - tle Child, __ Bye - bye, __ lul - le, __ lul - lay; __ Lul - lay, __ Thou ti - ny lit - tle Child, __ Bye - bye, __ lul - le, __ lul - lay.

Oh sis - ters two,_ how may_ we do_ To per - se - vere_ this

day?_____ To this_ poor Young - ling for whom we sing_ Bye - bye,_ lul - le,_ lul -

lay.

Her - od the King,_____ in_ his rag - ing, Charged_ he hath this day_____ His

sol - diers in __ their strength and might All chil - dren young to slay. _____ Then

woe __ is me __ poor child __ for Thee, __ And ev - er mourn __ and

say, _____ For at __ thy part - ing nor say nor sing __ Bye -

bye, __ lul - le, __ lul - lay.

And when the stars in gath - er do, In their far ven - ture stay, Then smile as dream - ing, Lit - tle One, Bye - bye, lul - le, lul - lay, bye - bye, lul - le, lul - lay.

MARY HAD A BABY
(Christmas Spiritual)

African-American Spiritual
arranged by Hall Johnson

*Johnson suggests singing the response "Yes, Lord" only in the verses beginning with the title.

D.S. al Fine

MARY'S SOLILOQUY

from the cantata *The St. Luke Christmas Story*

Lucy Vessey

Cecil Effinger

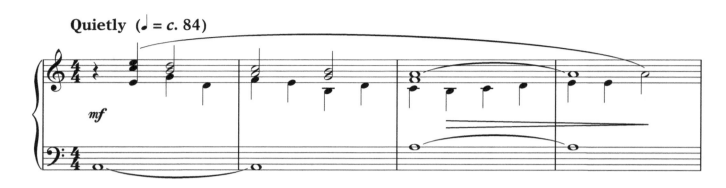

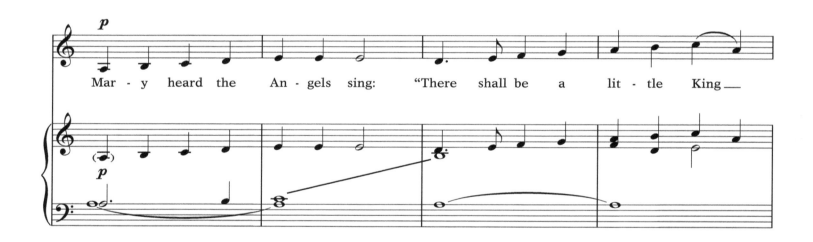

Mar - y heard the An - gels sing: "There shall be a lit - tle King

born to you, And He shall be ___ Great - er than all roy - al - ty."

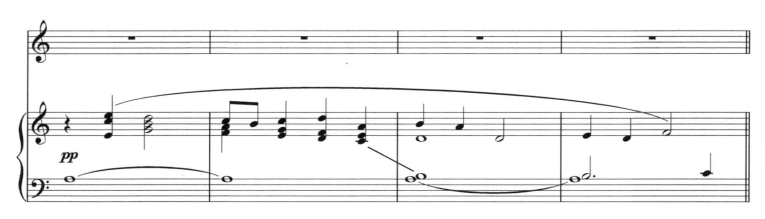

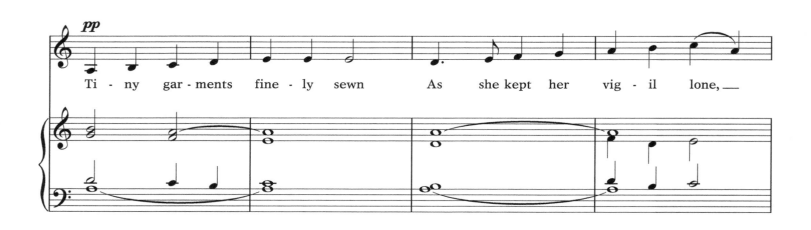

Ti - ny gar - ments fine - ly sewn As she kept her vig - il lone, __

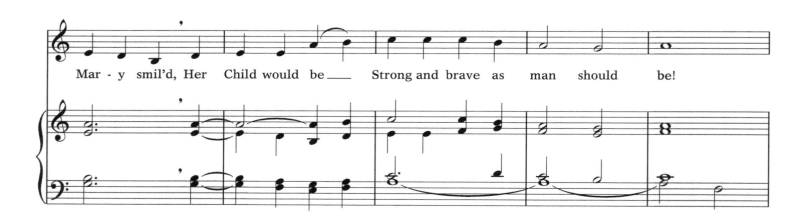

Mar - y smil'd, Her Child would be __ Strong and brave as man should be!

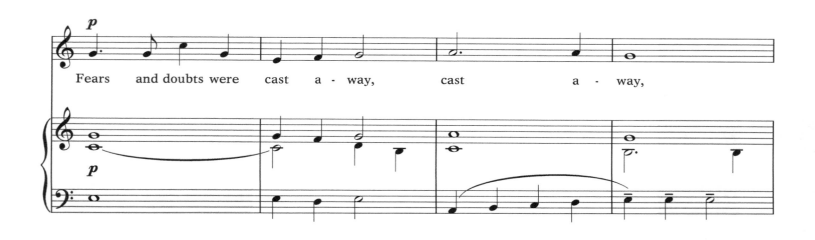

Fears and doubts were cast a - way, cast a - way,

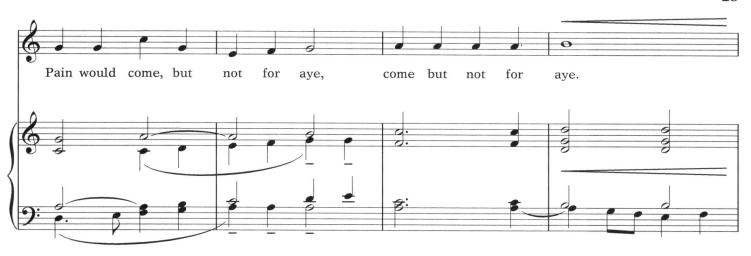

Pain would come, but not for aye, come but not for aye.

All would be for gain, not loss. Mar-y saw be-yond the cross,

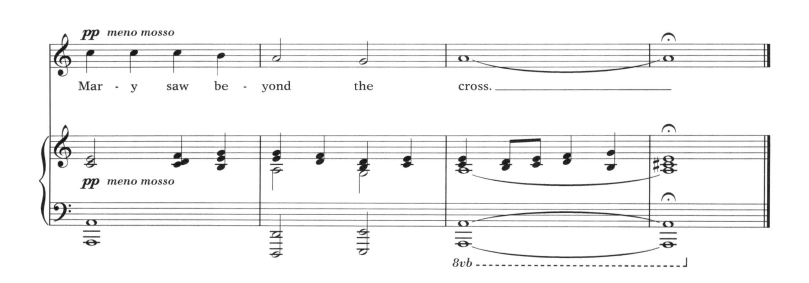

Mar-y saw be-yond the cross.

NOËL, NOËL, BELLS ARE RINGING

Alice Grainger★

Wilbur Chenoweth

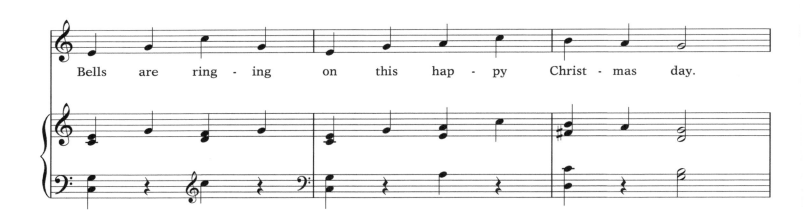

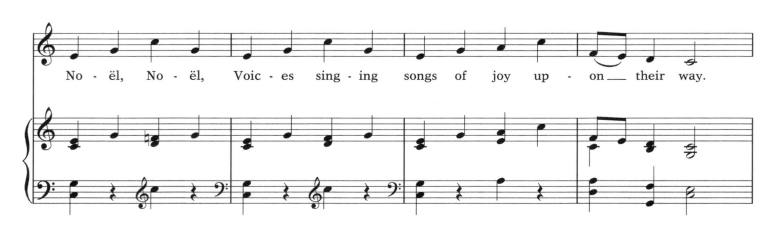

*Words used by special permission.

No - ël, No - ël, Mu - sic wing - ing through the night in tones so clear.

May Thy love and peace a - bide on this hap - py Christ - mas tide.

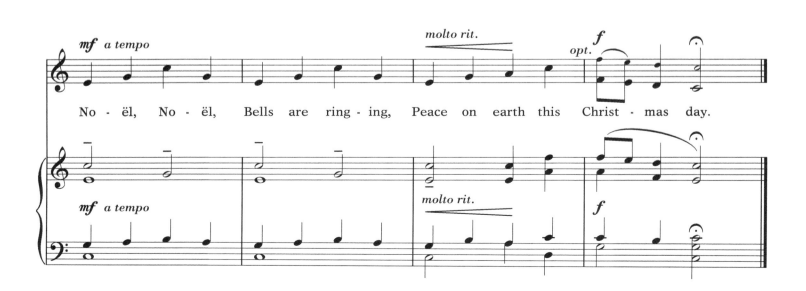

No - ël, No - ël, Bells are ring - ing, Peace on earth this Christ - mas day.

O HOLY NIGHT
(Cantique de Noël)

French Words by Placide Cappeau
English Words by John S. Dwight

Adolphe Adam

ON CHRISTMAS EVE
from *Five Christmas Songs*

Zacharias Topelius
English translation by Albert J. Hjerpe

Jean Sibelius
Op. 1, No. 3

SWEET LITTLE BOY JESUS

Words and Music by
John Jacob Niles

Very gently

1. Sweet lit-tle boy Je - sus in man-ger so low,____ Sweet
2. No place for the Moth - er, no place for the Son,____ No

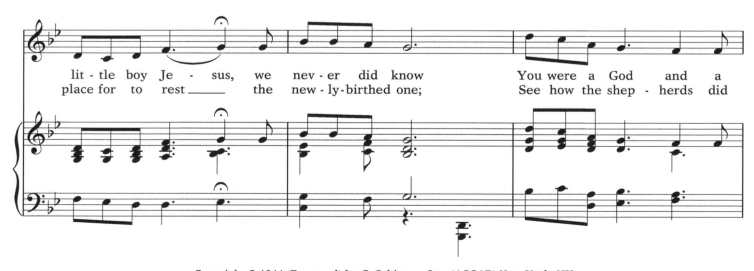

lit - tle boy Je - sus, we nev-er did know You were a God and a
place for to rest____ the new - ly-birthed one; See how the shep - herds did

39

WHAT CHILD IS THIS?

William C. Dix

"Greensleeves"
Old English Melody
arranged by Ernst Victor Wolff

What

Child is this, — who, laid to rest, On Ma-ry's lap — is sleep - ing? Whom

an - gels greet — with an - thems sweet, While shep - herds watch — are keep - ing?

This, this is Christ the King, Whom shep - herds guard and an - gels sing:

Haste, haste to bring Him laud, The Babe, the Son of

Ma - ry. Why lies He in such

mean es - tate Where ox and ass are feed - ing? Good

WHAT SONGS WERE SUNG

Words and Music by
John Jacob Niles

Tenderly ♩ = c. 66 *(in a story-telling manner)*

We can-not tell, we do not know What stars shone down so __ long a-go, When Mar-y birthed her own sweet Son And __ peace and love be-came as one. The Son of God, as scrip-tures said, Was Vir-gin born in a ti-ny shed, Where sim-ple shep-herds